LOST SHEEP AND BLUE SHUTTERS

The perils and pleasures of life in rural France

BY HELEN CHANDLER

THIS BOOK IS DEDICATED

TO CHRISTINE, WHO INSPIRED ME TO WRITE IT

INTRODUCTION

T his book tells the story of how I set off to start a new life in rural Brittany, with just my two cats and a few belongings. On arrival, I found not only my "house with blue shutters" but so much more.

The story was originally written for my own amusement and that of my family and friends. I hope, however, that others will enjoy reading it and laughing at my mistakes and misconceptions, my mangling of the French language and my moments of acute embarrassment. With hindsight I can see they were all part of the biggest learning curve of my life – and the biggest adventure. If you should decide to embark on a similar adventure, I wish you luck… and I am sure it will be just as exciting, and as much fun, as mine has been.

The stories in this book are true; the people in them are real. I have not changed any of the names because I am sure – generous souls that they are – that my lovely French neighbours, friends and students would have no objection to being included in this book. I will always remember them with the deepest affection and hope that they too will have some fond memories of *la petite Anglaise* with the cats and the funny accent, to whom they showed such unfailing kindness.

CHAPTER ONE

NEW BEGINNINGS

I have always loved stone houses with shutters. There would come a day, I promised myself, when I would buy a lovely old house with blue shutters and settle there with my cats to "live the dream". Somewhere in the heart of the countryside – maybe even beautiful, rural Brittany. One day...

I have met many people who had planned to move abroad – mostly France or Spain – but were overtaken by events before they could do so. Health problems or other complications had got in their way and the opportunity to live out their dreams had passed. So, after some consideration, I decided to seize the day and to do it while I could (and before I bottled out). In due course my little cottage on the Sussex coast went on the market and I began making plans for the big adventure.

Selling in the UK and buying in France simultaneously would have been extremely complicated, so I decided to do things in stages. Rented accommodation in Brittany was easy enough to find – holiday gites standing empty in the winter months were often available at a reasonable rent – so I soon found somewhere to stay in comfort while looking for a permanent home.

On a cold January day in 2007, I set off for Brittany with all my worldly goods tied up in a spotted handkerchief... Well of course, it wasn't quite like that, but I did take very little with me. Furniture and other items had been given away, sold, recycled or taken to the tip, while my few remaining effects were packed into bin-bags and cardboard boxes. I was thankful that my tendency towards minimalism (and my lack of cash) had prevented me from buying and hoarding loads of "stuff" which I would have to get rid of. Travelling light, I have always believed, is the way to go.

When the big day arrived, I packed my cats (in a large travelling cage), my bicycle, several bags and boxes and a few sundry items into the back of a small van, which a dear friend had volunteered to drive, and we headed for the ferry port at Portsmouth.

That evening, as the boat set off on its crossing to Saint-Malo, I remember looking back at the illuminated coastline and the dark water sparkling brightly with reflected lights. Too excited about this new adventure to feel sad, I still found it strange to think that, for the foreseeable future, England would no longer be my home.

Two days later, I was waving goodbye to my friend as he set off for the journey back to the UK, to return the hired van and the borrowed cat cage. During those two days, we had shopped to stock up the fridge, freezer and store cupboard, and explored a little of the surrounding area. Now, alone in my new rented home, I realised with a lurch in my stomach that it was all down to me now. The adventure had begun...

I soon settled into my temporary accommodation. The cats, Pip and Lucy - showing admirable resilience - appeared none the worse for their scary night-time voyage and wasted no time in investigating their new surroundings. I bought myself a little Renault Clio and set off to do some exploring of my own.

I was unsure at this point exactly which part of Brittany I would choose to buy a house – in those days property was still incredibly cheap and, even after paying off my UK mortgage, I had plenty of options available within my budget. I only knew I needed to be not too far from Brittany's capital, Rennes, for easy access to the airport and to maximise my chances of finding work – still in my early fifties, I would not have the option of retirement for some time yet. So I systematically explored the area around Rennes, then registered with an estate agency in Fougères, asking them to show me some properties.

What I was looking for, I explained in my best French, was one of those lovely old stone houses – with blue shutters of course – in a nice rural area. The agent I dealt with was a delightful and polite young man, who dutifully noted my requirements. Looking back now, I can imagine the thoughts going through his mind as I described my dream home. Phrases such as "money pit" and "freezing in winter" were no doubt swiftly followed by "is she mad?" and "well yes, she *is* English..." However, to his credit, he promised to make a list of all the properties in his portfolio which might be suitable and to assist me with my search.

Every couple of days, he would take me out in his car to view possible properties. I am a person who is not difficult to please, I know my own mind and I had expected to make my decision almost immediately. Somehow, though, none of the houses I saw were quite right. On paper they fitted my wish list but – it was impossible to say exactly why – I just couldn't see myself living in them. The old stone houses (many with their shutters painted in the traditional Breton blue) either needed a huge amount of work or were stuck in the middle of farmland, where the world and his tractor would have right of way across my land. Sensing my growing disappointment, the estate agent kindly reassured me that it can take time to find the perfect house. Sooner or later, he told me with a smile, I would feel the *"coup de foudre"* everyone has when they see the home of their dreams. I hadn't heard this expression before, but my dictionary told me it meant "love at first sight" which I thought was a wonderfully French attitude to house hunting.

After a couple of weeks of searching, on a bright, sunny day in early March, my patient and long suffering agent once again took me on a little tour of possible properties. Once again, there was nothing to quite fit the bill. Hesitantly, he told me there was one other property he could show me – it had just come onto the market – but he realised it didn't meet the criteria I had specified. Much newer than the other houses he had shown me, this one was built in the 1960s, in the *pavillon* style so beloved of the French – a sort of raised bungalow with a balcony and a large basement area.

He had been so helpful and polite that – although I was sure this "newer house" would be totally wrong for me in every way – I felt it would be churlish to refuse. So, with a sinking heart, I agreed to view it.

We pulled up at the big front gate and he stood back to let me walk down the drive and get my first sight of the house. In theory, it was a non-starter. This was not the old-style, stone-built house I had set my heart on. On going inside, it soon became clear that a new kitchen and bathroom – even by my non-exacting standards – would be needed. There was no wood-burning stove, another thing on my wish list. It didn't really tick any of the boxes. The shutters were not even blue. And yet…

I started asking questions. Was there the possibility of installing a wood-burner? Inspecting the flue configuration, the estate agent told me yes, there was. Might the vendors consider an offer, so I could keep back some of my budget for the work required? He was sure they would.

Outside again, I looked all around. Twice the size of my old home in the UK, the house stood in about a third of an acre of private land with fruit trees and a large grassy area at the back. Four pairs of French windows on the south side of the house opened onto a pretty balcony overhung with peach trees; a sloping terrace was filled with flowering shrubs. The wooden shutters, currently white, could easily be painted blue… and that view! Wow. Just wow.

All around was beautiful open countryside. In the garden, daffodils and purple crocuses provided a vivid splash of colour and, to complete this rural idyll, tiny lambs frisked in the adjacent field, baa-ing sweetly.

Having patiently allowed me to stand there for a few minutes taking it all in, the estate agent approached me with a satisfied smile. Noting the soppy grin on my face, he must have been saying to himself "job done!" (and to the lambs, "I'll pay you later, chaps").

Standing by my side, he looked from me to the house, then back at me. The soppy grin was still there.

"Le coup de foudre, madame?" he asked gently.

I could find no words, in French or in English, to tell him what I knew, beyond a shadow of a doubt: this house was destined to become my home.

All I could manage, weakly, was a one word answer.

"Oui."

CHAPTER TWO

MEETING THE NEIGHBOURS

By the end of May, the cats and I were safely installed in the house with the not-yet-blue shutters and quickly made ourselves at home. The house formed part of a small hamlet, a group of houses on either side of a winding country road, some distance apart compared to what I was used to, but close enough not to feel too isolated.

The walk to the little village took about twenty minutes, passing a granite quarry and some very pretty countryside. The village centre comprised - at that point - a convenience store, a post office, a *boulangerie*, the mayor's offices, a small library, a church and two bars. It was very small and very French.

As for my neighbours, I learnt that some were French and some English, and I looked forward to making the acquaintance of them all in due course.

Meanwhile, it was a treat just to wake up every day to the peace and tranquility of the beautiful rural setting and to lie in bed at night listening to the sounds of the countryside. Owls and foxes calling in the distance lulled me to sleep; I awoke to the sound of birdsong. As for the house, in my (totally unbiased) opinion, it was perfect. With its newly fitted kitchen and bathroom, I considered it more beautiful than ever and, once I had made a good start on the interior decorating, I turned my attention to some outside jobs.

"Ooooouur house," I sang happily, sloshing blue paint onto the wooden shutters, *"is a very, very, very fine house... with two cats*

in the yaaaard…" The two cats exchanged eloquent glances and moved hastily out of earshot.

I had chosen a patch of land at the front of the house for a vegetable garden; it was to be a proper little French *potager*. The previous owners had it all grassed over – an ideal play area for their grandchildren – so for its change of use, the ground would need turning over before I started.

On a sunny day, I set out with my garden fork and spade and prepared to dig. Arbitrarily choosing my starting point, I attempted to thrust the fork into the ground. Nothing happened. I tried again, then again using my new spade. Its sharp, shiny edge didn't even break the surface.

At this point, to my acute embarrassment, my lovely French neighbour Raymond turned up. He smiled kindly at me over the low garden wall, watching my futile efforts with sympathy.

"C'est dur, Hélène!" he pointed out unnecessarily. *"C'est trop dur!"*

I smiled politely back at him, thinking, *yes I know it's too flipping hard!*

Determined not to be written off as an English wimp, I raised the fork with a flourish and, as my neighbour watched with interest, I thrust it into the ground once again with all my might – then, for good measure, I stood on it. Nothing. I jumped on it, as hard as I could. It didn't move. I fell off.

"Oui," I conceded at last, *"c'est trop dur"*.

My neighbour walked away, clucking sympathetically, to reappear moments later with a scrap of paper on which was written a name and a phone number. Someone he knew, he told me tactfully, had a rotavator. He wondered if it might be of interest?…

Filled with relief, I shook his hand warmly (we would soon progress to four kisses, but more of that later). As I thanked him profusely, he brushed off my gratitude with a smile and a typically French *"de rien, de rien"* – not at all, it's nothing!

Before leaving me nursing the scrap of paper and my bruised pride, he told me kindly, "Mention my name when you phone him – he'll give you a special rate!"

The little vegetable plot having been duly rotavated, I set about planting my crops. I had started a selection of seedlings in pots on my sunny balcony and, once they were large enough, I began to bed them out in the freshly dug earth. Tomatoes, courgettes, beans and sweetcorn were the first.

My gardening efforts were a rich source of entertainment to my nearest neighbour, Henri. An elderly man with an insatiable curiosity and an incomprehensible accent – if you listen to *The Archers,* imagine a French Joe Grundy – he would stand at my garden gate while I worked, alternately mumbling and bellowing at me. He could have been delivering encouragement, advice or comments on the weather – I could never be quite sure which, so I simply smiled politely and nodded, hopefully in the right places.

On one occasion when I did manage to understand him, he asked me what crops I was planting. Quite glad to take a break for a moment, I leaned on my spade and listed them for him. The last one, *maïs doux* (sweetcorn), is something I've always had trouble pronouncing, but I gave it my best shot. Henri looked at me blankly. I repeated the words and tried to explain. It was yellow, I told him, a real delicacy, you could eat it raw or cooked. The plants grew high, I went on, warming to my theme and pantomiming something a little taller than me. They were delicious and very – er – yellow, I finished lamely. Henri, looking suspicious, pondered this for a moment, then his face lit up and he cried *"ah – maïs doux!"* Which was what I thought I had said, but evidently not. Open mouthed, he looked at me as if I was mad.

"Maïs doux?" he repeated in disbelief. *"Maïs doux!!* And the English eat this? *Pffftt!!* We grow it in the fields for cattle fodder!" Muttering to himself about the culinary vagaries of *les Anglais*, he

stomped off in disgust. Well, that told me.

Over time, my ears grew more accustomed to the local accent and my conversations with Henri became a little less challenging. He appeared to be obsessed, for some reason, with the British royal family. He would ask me if I knew that the Queen's husband, the Prince Philippe, was ill, or that "Lady Di's son" William was to be married. Had I met the Queen Elizabeth? he wanted to know. What was she like? One day, a little frustrated at being bombarded with questions as I was trying to tend my runner beans, I pointed out that France had once had its own royalty – and, I added darkly, look what the French had done to *them*!

"*Pffft!*" replied Henri quickly, brushing off my allusion to *La Révolution*. "That was different!"

I never mentioned it again.

Henri's wife, Chantal, some years younger than him, is one of the kindest people I have ever met. She would happily describe herself as *costaude* (tough and sturdy) and worked in the garden with an energy that put me to shame, even in the later years when Henri became too old and frail to do his share and Chantal herself needed a hip replacement. Unfailingly cheerful, she would always ask me how things were going and make me promise to let her know if I needed help with anything. On the occasions when I took her up on this kind offer, she would always brush off my thanks, saying, "*Ca s'appelle le voisinage!*" It's called being neighbours.

I discovered that the lambs (and their mothers) belonged to Chantal. A new batch of them would appear each year in early spring; they would be moved around from one piece of pasture to another, including the land next to my garden where I had first seen them. (As a vegetarian, I preferred to enjoy their company every spring without dwelling too much on their inevitable fate). It was an enchanting sight to see Chantal, looking every inch the nursery rhyme shepherdess with her crook, rounding up the sheep and persuading them to follow her.

The pace of life was slow. Breton people, I discovered, could not or would not be hurried. An example of this is the four kisses I mentioned earlier. As a reserved Brit, my normal greeting on seeing someone is either to shake their hand or simply say hello, depending on how well I know them and the formality of the occasion. The French, however, like kissing – and in rural Brittany four kisses to greet someone is the norm. In some other regions, two kisses are considered sufficient, but here in Brittany, where they take their time over everything, things are done differently.

Raymond was the first one to teach me this. Once we had got to know each other, every time we met I would receive a series of four kisses, or *bisous* – one on each cheek, then repeat. This, I discovered, was the traditional Breton greeting between neighbours and friends. I have to admit that in the early days I found this rather disconcerting. On more than one occasion I pulled away too soon, leaving the kisser puckered up expectantly, so that I had to go back for the other two. I began to feel a little stressed every time I saw someone making a beeline for me, lips pursed in readiness. What if they weren't from Brittany and only wanted two kisses, while I tried to give them four? Until you get used to it, it can be a bit of a minefield. In time I became quite an expert on "French kissing" (so to speak) but on my visits back to the UK, I found I had to restrain myself from delivering a batch of four with great gusto every time I met someone.

Taking their time is what the Breton people do best. No matter how pressed for time you or they may be, they will greet you, kiss you and embark on the obligatory pleasantries before any meaningful exchanges can begin. How was the house coming along? they would ask. The garden? The little cats? Have you found work yet? How are your family in England?... and so on. Normally this quaint Breton custom was very endearing, but it could present problems. I discovered this one sunny spring afternoon as I stood on the balcony of my house with a bucket of water and a cloth, cleaning my four pairs of French windows.

All was tranquil and serene; the only sound was birdsong. The sun, high in a brilliant blue sky, made my windows sparkle satisfyingly. At peace with the world, I paused momentarily to enjoy the view, gazing down at my large back garden to admire the grassy slopes and the fruit trees. I did a double-take. Several ewes and their lambs were happily munching my grass. There was a gap at the bottom of Chantal's fence which they had managed to limbo underneath, to sample what my garden had to offer. Like beasts and people the world over, they clearly believed that the grass was greener on the other side.

For a moment I stood transfixed, watching them with some amusement. As they became aware of my presence, the lambs started bouncing up and down, bleating in their high little voices. Their mothers, looking up crossly from their free meal, glared at me disapprovingly, daring me to go near their precious babies. It was all rather sweet, I thought, such a lovely, rural scene. However, I would need to let Chantal know...

At this point, one of the more adventurous animals left the grass and tottered onto the driveway, which led towards the front gate and – oh no – my vegetable patch. Thinking of all the tender plants growing there, so lovingly nurtured and now destined to be ravaged and devoured by rogue sheep, I knew I must act quickly. Even now, the rest of the flock, seeing their friend plodding determinedly up the drive, were beginning to follow her like – er – sheep.

Falling over the bucket of soapy water in my haste, I rushed up the drive and out of the gate which I shut firmly to prevent the escapees from getting onto the road, then ran as fast as I could to Chantal's house. As her kindly face appeared at the door, I began to blurt out my story – but I had forgotten my Breton manners. Politely but firmly, after bestowing on me the obligatory four kisses, she led me indoors to meet the family.

Her daughter, son-in-law, grandson and a family friend were seated at a large table strewn with the remains of a good lunch.

With smiles and cries of delight, they all got up to greet me, kissing me four times each and asking – as Breton people do – about my health, my house, my cats. How kind of me to visit! Would I please join them for a little coffee? They were just about to make a fresh pot...

Surfacing between bouts of kissing, I attempted to explain the dire circumstances.

"The sheep - " I began.

"We have tea if you prefer it," they offered thoughtfully.

"You see, they're in my - "

"We know how you English love your tea!" Winks and indulgent smiles all round.

"But they're going to – if we don't - "

"Sugar's on the table – help yourself, Hélène! So lovely to see you! Now, tell us all about - "

At this point, a thudding and creaking noise above us made me look up. Henri, bleary-eyed from his afternoon nap, was plodding down the stairs to find out what all the fuss was about.

"Hélène!" he greeted me with delight, puckering up in anticipation. On no, I thought, please no. The kissing was going to start all over again. Meanwhile, my lettuces were being reduced to stumps and my prize tomatoes were – well, it didn't even bear thinking about. Before Henri had time to lunge at me I decided that, manners or no manners, I would have to take control of the situation.

"Your sheep" I announced loudly and without pausing for breath "have escaped from your field and they're in my garden and if we don't stop them they're going to eat everything in my vegetable patch!"

There was a momentary silence as everyone present considered the grave implications of this statement. Then Chantal reached for her shepherd's crook with one hand, patting my arm gently with the other.

"*Ma puce,*" she said kindly, "Sweetheart. Why didn't you tell us that in the first place?..."

The story – for my vegetables at least – had a happy ending. The sheep, before spotting my pampered plants, had discovered that they could run all the way round the house, return to the back garden, eat a bit more grass, then head up the drive again, go round the house... and so on. The ewes were happily engaged in this exciting game when we found them. The lambs were watching them, bouncing and squeaking with delight, for all the world like children cheering on their mums in the parents' race on sports day.

Chantal, with a stern word and a wave of her crook, rounded up the flock of miscreants and led them away to safety. Her border fence was repaired the following day. The sheep's adventures were over – and my vegetables had lived to fight another day.

CHAPTER THREE

LEARNING TO FIT IN

O n arriving in France I thought my French was pretty good – I
had studied it to "A" level and had worked as a bilingual sec-
retary in the UK. However, I soon realized that "school French" is
one thing, whereas what the French people actually speak is another thing altogether.

My first real introduction to French swearing came quite early
on, by courtesy of my other nearest neighbours – a retired French
couple living on the other side of me – and their "*palets* parties".
I had never before heard of *palets* but soon discovered that this
traditional French game was extremely popular in Brittany. It is
a game of skill in which players throw cast iron discs onto a soft-
wood board. Or so I am told. To my neighbours and their friends
– surprisingly rowdy for a group of pensioners – it seemed to be
more an excuse for a booze-up on a Sunday afternoon, involving a
lot of shouting and swearing.

I will always remember the first time I heard a "*palets* party" taking place. I was sunbathing on my balcony one Sunday afternoon,
relaxing with a nice cup of tea, surveying the peach trees loaded
with fruit and thinking how peaceful it was living in the countryside. Then the noises began. *Clunk. Thud. Clunk.* I deduced
that some sort of game was being played from the accompanying
cheers and yells of *tant mieux* – good for you! – or groans of disappointment when, presumably, a *clunk* had landed in the wrong
place. It was all very civilised and the sounds were actually quite
soporific, wafting on the summer air through a screen of trees.
Leaning back on my sun-lounger, watching a red squirrel scamper

along my garden wall, I sipped my tea happily. There was a certain vicarious pleasure to be had from listening to the sounds of French people enjoying their weekend.

Then things started to get competitive. The match was clearly heating up. The initial polite, sporting cries of *zut!* and *oh la la!* gave way to more earthy vocabulary. Some of these words I was already familiar with, some I found later by researching them in an online dictionary. Others were apparently altogether too rude to be included in "Google Translate" and I can only assume they constituted some rather colourful Breton oaths not normally used in polite company.

In the middle of all this, I became aware of somebody shouting something about a cow.

"La vache!" they cried. Then, more loudly and on a note of deep disappointment, *"Oh, la vache!"*

Puzzled, I looked around. The piece of pasture land which lay between my garden and that of my neighbours was indeed often used for grazing by the local farmer's cows. These were slow, dozy and harmless creatures to whom I would often chat as I pottered in the garden. Today, however, there was not a cow in sight. Very strange indeed...

"La vache!" came another voice, followed by groans of commiseration from some, laughter and cheers from others. My curiosity piqued, I looked all around again. Still no cows. Had one of them, I wondered, perhaps escaped from wherever it had been put to graze (memories of the sheep episode still came back to haunt me) and was it even now marauding around my neighbours' garden and ruining their game?

So it went on, the elusive cow having her name taken in vain from time to time throughout the afternoon, until the game finally ended and the visitors, rosy-cheeked with Calvados, piled into their cars and went home.

Shortly afterwards, I told some French friends about this puzzling episode. They laughed until they cried. "Don't you know?" they giggled. "Have you never heard that before?"

Feeling rather foolish, I admitted that I hadn't. They were delighted to put me right.

"La vache!", I learned, was a common and very versatile French expression, used for conveying shock, disgust, disappointment and a number of other emotions. Its meaning – roughly translated into English – was "oh hell!" or maybe "b*gger it!"

The cow mystery was solved and my education was complete.

Grasping the intricacies of the French language was not the only cultural challenge I was to encounter. I soon discovered that the ethos of rural Brittany was similar in many ways to the 1950s and early 1960s I remembered from my childhood. This could be delightful – the slower pace of life meant less stress, people were more polite and always had time to chat (and kiss). Children's manners were, on the whole, exemplary; senior citizens were treated with kindness and respect; people looked out for each other.

However, this "time warp" also had its disadvantages. Women, for example, were regarded by many men – in the rural areas at least – as second class citizens. Single women in particular were looked at askance (especially those who, like me, had the temerity to be happy in their single state). I discovered this on numerous occasions and, after being initially irritated and puzzled, I later learned to treat this bigotry as the joke that it is.

I will never forget the day when I answered a knock at the door to find a tradesman standing on my doorstep. Did Madame know, he asked me, that there was moss on her roof? My roof was a relatively new one and seemed to me to be in good condition, but as I was about to point this out, the man went on to explain that he was a professional cleaner of roofs and would be happy to remove all my moss at a very reasonable rate.

Having listened politely to his "spiel", I thanked him and replied that I didn't require his services at the moment, but if he would like to leave a flyer or business card…

At this point I realised that the tradesman was no longer listening to me. With a distracted air, he was looking over my shoulder into the hallway behind me. Feeling rather uneasy, I resisted the temptation to look round – there was, after all, no-one else in the house. Instead, I smiled encouragingly, hoping to get his attention back.

His next words quickly wiped the smile from my face.

"Can't I discuss it with your husband?"

Several possible replies to this sprang to mind, but I didn't feel that any of them would adequately do justice to what I was thinking. I could of course just say no, but then he might have suggested that maybe there was some other male relative lurking around (a toddler grandson, perhaps) who could speak on my behalf. However, I was spared the trouble of replying - the look on my face must have shown him, more clearly than words, the error of his ways. Backing away with a muttered *bonne journée* the man beat a hasty retreat.

Strangely enough, he didn't even leave his business card.

If there's one thing the French understand even less than a happy and confident single woman, it's a vegetarian. Once again, I was reminded of the 50s and 60s in Britain, when such people were whispered about and regarded as very strange indeed. These days, of course, nobody in the UK bats an eyelid if you mention it. In England I do still get asked questions sometimes – for example, is it for the benefits to health and to the environment, or animal welfare concerns? (the latter, in my case, while the former are an added bonus) – but in general people just seem politely interested or, at the very least, accepting of the fact that we all have the right to live the lifestyle we choose. Not so in rural France.

While not being the world's greatest cook, I still enjoy making my "veggie" meals from scratch most of the time. However, there are days when there's nothing like a supermarket ready-meal, or a meat-free burger, when you're feeling tired or lazy or just want something easy to prepare.

I soon found that no such equivalent products were available in the local supermarkets. My polite enquiries were met with blank looks and shrugs. Restaurant staff, I discovered, could get quite huffy if you requested an alternative to meat or fish. On one occasion I asked if it might be possible to have an omelette – a plain one would be fine, I said, with my best ingratiating smile – but the reply was an uncompromising "*non*" and I had to be content with a bowl of chips. (I suspected these had been cooked in animal fat but decided it would be unwise to question it.) Since food is, in my opinion, one of life's great pleasures – and France is supposedly world famous for its magnificent cuisine – I pondered many times on this anomaly. I finally concluded that as far as the French, at least in Brittany, were concerned, food was indeed to be enjoyed – but only one sort of diet was permitted. It consisted of meat, meat and, er, more meat.

I soon learned that mentioning vegetarianism in Brittany is not a good idea. Reactions, when I did so, were varied. Some people looked uncomfortable and sidled hastily away from me. Some patted my arm sympathetically, murmuring "you poor thing" and similar platitudes. One lady looked genuinely horrified, clapping her hand over her mouth with a shocked "*mon Dieu!*"

Intrigued by the devastating affect the "V word" was having on people, I asked a trusted French friend the reason why.

"Oh, that's simple!" she replied with a shrug. "In France – well, the rural parts anyway – a lot of people consider vegetarianism to be a mental illness."

Ah, well. That would explain everything.

It took several years for me to get to grips with these foibles, quirks and prejudices and to learn what it is safe to say and to whom without fear of repercussions. At the beginning of my life in France, however, there was a much more pressing consideration. After buying the house, the car and the new kitchen and bathroom (oh yes, and the wood-burning stove!) the remainder of my funds still represented a fairly substantial sum, but this was not going to last forever. As soon as possible, I would have to find work.

Had I known how difficult this would be, I might have thought twice about coming to Brittany. However, here I was and here I would stay, for the foreseeable future. So work of some description would have to be found.

With a wealth of experience in admin and secretarial work in the UK, plus the added bonus (or so I thought) of fluency in two languages and a good knowledge of business French, I reckoned I could find an office job in France without too much difficulty. I soon realised that this was not the case. Any posts requiring an English speaker, such as office staff in estate agents or banks, were immediately taken by bright school leavers with excellent language grades in their *baccalauréat.* I could only wish them well, reflecting wryly that within a few years they would probably be bank managers or have their own estate agencies. In many cases they were almost young enough to be my grandchildren. It was all rather depressing.

Still, I reminded myself, what is an adventure without challenges? Casting my job-seeking net a little wider, I was lucky enough to get several short-term contracts. Waitressing, cleaning hotel rooms, packing vegetables – I was happy to try almost anything – but the work was tiring and poorly paid. Once, to my delight, I got a three-month contract working on the beautiful

Mont St-Michel, making various fillings and stuffing them into baguettes. My French improved, my resilience increased... but the pay was never more than the minimum wage permitted by law – and my goodness, we worked hard for it.

Around this time I also started doing a little tele-sales work for an "ex-pat" website (some in English, some in French) this being another useful experience I had had in the UK. It proved fairly lucrative and things improved for a while, but the earnings were intermittent, with some good weeks and some bad. I needed to supplement it with some regular – and better paid – work.

Life, so the great John Lennon once observed, is what happens while you are busy making other plans. I was soon to discover the truth of this. While I was frantically scouring the job vacancies in the local newspaper and on the internet, fate had a surprise in store for me. A career change in my mid 50s was the last thing I had expected, but it remains one of the best things ever to have happened to me. This is how it all came about.

I had been introduced to a French couple, some years younger than me, who often invited me to their house. They both spoke excellent English but were also kind enough to allow me to practise my less than excellent French on them.

One day, at the time of my unproductive job search, this couple told me that a friend of theirs, Patrick – a local garage owner – had decided to take English lessons. *Tant mieux!* was my immediate reaction. Good for him! Exchanging conspiratorial looks, my friends went on to break the news that they had recommended my services to him as a teacher.

More than a little shocked, I replied politely but firmly that I had never been a teacher, had no desire ever to become a teacher, and hoped *monsieur le garagiste* would find a suitable pedagogue to meet his requirements.

When I next met these friends, they broached the subject again: would I please meet Patrick and discuss plans for the commencement of his English lessons? Rather more firmly this time, I reiterated my previous response, in both languages for added emphasis: "Sorry, but no! *Désolée, mais non!*" Just to make it quite clear, you see, no misunderstandings.

To this my friends replied – rather too casually for my liking – that they had invited their *garagiste* friend and his lovely wife Roseline to dinner the following week and (surprise!) that I was invited to come along too – just to meet them, no obligation obviously... and *if* he should ask me about the teaching – well, then I could explain to him myself that the proposed lessons were not going to happen.

On the day of the dinner, I arrived in full assertiveness mode, ready to make it clear that *"non"* means *"non"*. However, as the evening progressed, I found myself totally disarmed by this delightful and devoted couple to whom I took an instant liking (*"on se tutoie?"* they asked me after we had exchanged kisses – shall we use the informal *"tu"* when we speak to each other?)

Patrick explained that he only remembered a few words of English from his school days (which were nearly as long ago as mine) but that he had bought a grammar book and just needed some help getting to grips with the finer points of the English language. His ideal teacher would be someone who was conversant with French grammar as well as English (to facilitate explanations) and who would have patience with an almost complete beginner... Suffice it to say that by the end of the evening we had fixed a date – the following Tuesday at 7pm – for the first (trial) lesson, which I promised would be free (in case my worst suspicions were founded and I made a rubbish teacher).

Thus I acquired my first and most dearly loved student. From struggling to string a few words together beyond "hello" and "how are you?" he became more and more at ease chatting in English. As his fluency and confidence grew, so too did his clientele of British customers, who would recommend his garage to each other. Hearing people talk about that nice bloke in Fougères who spoke such excellent English, I would feel immensely proud.

Finally – after several years of lessons – Patrick told me that he and his wife had sold the garage, were about to start their retirement and were planning to travel the world, something I knew they had been thinking about for some time. His English lessons were therefore coming to an end.

At his last lesson we reminisced, as old friends do, over *Kouign Amman* (my favourite Breton cake) and a couple of beers, talking of the future and the past, promising to stay in touch (which we have). Over the years, we had shared good times and bad: the arrival of grandchildren and loss of a parent (his), the deaths of beloved cats and of near neighbours (mine), as well as many anecdotes about our lives and friends. My cats adored him and friends from the UK would make sure that their visits to me coincided with a Tuesday, so as not to miss Patrick. So yes, that final lesson was not without its sadness – but as Patrick said, "this is not *adieu*, only *au revoir*".

I still laugh about some of his not-quite-right colloquialisms and slightly unusual interpretations of English expressions. The best by a mile was the "brothel" episode. I should explain at this point that I had not, at the time, encountered the not very polite French expression *"c'est le bordel!"* which roughly translates as "it's an awful mess!" Until, that is, one Tuesday evening when Patrick – currently busy with some messy DIY at his house – asked me "what is the English for *le bordel?*" Slightly taken aback, I replied that a *bordel*, in English, is called a brothel. Writing the word carefully in his exercise book, Patrick continued cheerfully, "Roseline and I invite you to dinner when our house is no longer a brothel"...

Other gems included expensive items costing "a leg and an arm" and his opinion that I had "the green hand" when complimenting me on my gardening efforts. A forget-me-not will forever more to me be a "don't-forget-me".

As Patrick's fluency improved, his conversation became liberally sprinkled with some of his favourite colloquialisms. Occasionally he might feel "under the weather". Vocabulary exercises were, to him, "a piece of cake", whereas irregular verbs were just "not his cup of tea".

I received another postcard this week from Patrick and Roseline, written in Patrick's idiomatic and almost perfect English, from one of the exciting places they are visiting all over the world. They are enjoying a full, happy and well deserved retirement and no doubt Patrick is using his English at every opportunity.

Adding the card to my colourful collection, I reflect that we never have any idea what fate has in store for us. If I had not met Patrick and his wife through mutual friends all those years ago, I would have missed out on the friendship of two lovely people – and I never would have discovered that teaching English was "just my cup of tea".

CHAPTER FOUR

A NEW CAREER

T eaching Patrick was not only very rewarding in itself – as well as great fun – but it led to other work. The progress of my "star pupil" was so good and the lessons so successful that I felt confident enough to respond to an advertisement from a teaching agency, with a client based in Rennes who needed to learn English for his job. More in hope than expectation, I wrote a *"lettre de motivation"* in my best French, explaining that, whilst having no formal qualifications, I was currently teaching (with great success) a professional gentleman who would, I felt sure, be happy to provide a reference.

To my astonishment, I got the job. To my delight, it all went well. To my bank manager's delight and astonishment, I was once again solvent.

Next time I saw a similar advert, I sent my CV and covering letter with a little more optimism, telling the agency that I was currently successfully teaching English to two professional gentlemen and that references could be provided if required. Again, I got the job.

A new career had begun...

◆ ◆ ◆

Over the next few years, most of my work comprised face-to-face lessons with professional individuals, so I was a little apprehensive about my first group lesson. The students were members of the twinning association of a nearby town. On a cold September evening, I turned up early at the old school building where the lessons were to take place. I was determined to be well prepared when my students arrived – first impressions are so important.

Unpacking my books in the big, draughty old classroom, I shivered – surely it was time to have the radiators on? I hoped it would warm up a little when a few people arrived.

On cue, I heard the door open. The keen student was about ten minutes early, but that didn't matter – I was ready to face the music. The newcomer was a middle aged man, on the short side – as Breton men often are – and dressed casually. Greeting him in English, with a big smile and a shake of the hand (the four kisses, I felt, might be a little premature at this stage), I invited him to come in and sit down.

"Bonsoir, madame," he replied a little uneasily. Poor chap, I thought, he's nervous. I must put him at his ease.

"Good evening," I said again, "nice to meet you! My name is Helen".

"Bonsoir," he muttered again.

This was going to be a challenge. At my interview, I had been told to expect the students to speak in English at all times. If they lapsed into French, I must reply to them in English. This, after all, was what I was there for.

"The others will be here in a moment," I continued encouragingly. "Then we can make a start."

The man eyed me suspiciously.

"Tell me" – I was gabbling now, beginning to realise that something was horribly wrong – "have you had English classes before?"

The man stood, drew himself up to his full five foot two and fixed me with an uncompromising stare.

"Madame," he said firmly and with great dignity, *"je suis le concierge".*

He had come to turn on the heating.

In the early days, when I was still building up my client base of adult students, I was lucky enough to get a job for one academic year as a part-time English assistant working in four different schools in Fougères. Three of these were primary schools, the other a secondary with pupils aged eleven and over. The older children were delightful – hard working, helpful and unfailingly courteous to me, with a lovely sense of humour – and their lessons were very rewarding. However, I have to confess that it was the little ones who really captured my heart. French children, I discovered, start learning English at a very early age. It was therefore my job and my great pleasure to assist the teachers of the *classe primaire* and even the *classe maternelle* in teaching the "tinies" some numbers, colours and a few basic phrases and instructions in English.

The little ones loved it – no grammar lessons for them, that would come soon enough. At that age, it was all just a game. I taught them songs and rhymes to help them remember numbers and words. They were very excited to have a real English person in their lessons and made a big fuss of me, running to greet me in the playground with the usual four kisses and an "Ello, Elen, 'ow are you?" I still smile at the memory of them singing "heads and shoulders, knees and toes" as we did the actions together, and remember the laughter and groans as they failed to listen carefully enough during games of "Simon Says".

The adult lessons – mostly in Rennes – were building up nicely at that time, and it was not uncommon for me to divide a working day between a couple of different schools and a trip to Rennes for one of the adults (not forgetting, of course, to be home in time for Patrick's lesson on a Tuesday evening). It was quite a demanding schedule, but – as any self-employed person knows – it makes sense to accept all work that comes your way, as it is frequently a "famine or feast" situation. At least I succeeded in keeping everyone happy and (as far as I can remember) never asked a professional person to sing after me "heads, shoulders, knees and toes" when I should have been testing them on irregular verbs.

By the time the school job ended, I had enough adult students to keep things ticking over and, apart from a few times when I gave *soutien scolaire* (extra tutoring) to teenagers who were struggling with their English lessons, I now focused on giving lessons solely to professional adults. These were extremely interesting people to work with, coming as they did from very diverse career backgrounds. I have taught computer experts, engineers, shop assistants, sales representatives and numerous others, with levels of English from elementary to advanced. All had different needs for their particular job; each one had his or her individual learning style; all worked hard although some were more motivated than others. One thing they all had in common: they hated irregular verbs with a passion.

Some of the older students (around my age and approaching retirement) were particularly fun to work with. They were often big fans of British and American music, frequently interrupting a lesson to tell me "I know that word! I heard it in a song by ...." etc.

Their love of pop and rock music did not, however, always do a great deal for their English. They would occasionally argue the toss with me about a grammar or syntax construction which they had "heard in a song, so it must be right". I remember a lovely student of around my age telling me with a deadpan expression, "I can't get no internet access today". I gently corrected him, but he was adamant that this must be right, quoting as proof the Rolling Stones' song "I can't get no satisfaction". As I began to point out, with some asperity, that it was I and not Mick Jagger who was giving him English lessons, I saw from the twinkle in his eye that he was indeed "taking the Mick" – out of his teacher...

Another older student, also looking forward to his retirement, was a keen guitarist - and, like me, was a huge fan of Bruce Springsteen. His level of English was very good, so instead of focussing on the finer points of grammar, I was happy for him to chat about Gibsons and Fenders and the sort of music he loved. His other great passion was travel; he would tell me about the places he and his wife had already visited and those they planned to explore once they were retired. At his last lesson with me – perhaps as a sort of "end of term" gesture – he wore jeans and a T-shirt bearing the motif *Born to Run*. I think of him whenever I hear that song, and hope that he and his wife are having a wonderful retirement, filled with adventures, travel... and lots of music.

All the people I worked with had their own story to tell and some of them were extremely interesting and unusual. One student, a lovely French-Vietnamese woman in her 30s, had a wonderful sense of humour and the most infectious laugh I have ever heard, which usually resulted in us both having fits of giggles at some point during her lessons. I discovered however that her start in life had been anything but funny. When I asked her once if she had lived in Rennes all her life, she replied no – in fact she hadn't even lived in France all her life. "Tell me more," I said without thinking. She explained that she had arrived with her parents in the late 1970s "on a boat". She didn't remember anything about it, she said, having been a baby of about eighteen months at the time. Listening to her story, I learned that her family had been among the tens of thousands of refugees who had fled their native land to seek safety in France, the UK and other countries – the Vietnamese "Boat People".

Looking serious for the first time ever, my student told me quietly "my parents never talk about it."

One of my favourite students was the founder and head of a thriving company near Rennes which specialised in computer systems and technology. This wealthy and extremely clever man, who was, I believe, in his mid-forties, had the most engaging manner and one of the most boyish grins I have ever seen. Every time I met him I had to restrain myself from straightening his tie and telling him not to miss the school bus. He was, quite simply, adorable, and knew just how to wrap his English teacher round his little finger.

One day, he asked me if it would be possible to change the time of his next lesson, which had been booked for the civilised hour of nine-thirty. It turned out that there was a meeting he needed to attend that morning and the only way he could do so and not miss his lesson would be if we started at seven-thirty instead. (Which would mean me leaving home around six forty-five, which would mean getting up at – well – silly o'clock...) My charming student was looking hopefully at me with a bashful and apologetic grin. That tie needed straightening again.

"Of course," I gulped. "No problem at all."

It was pitch dark when I left home and equally dark when I arrived at the offices shortly before seven-thirty. The car park, as I pulled into it, was empty, the office building in complete darkness. In the warmth of my car, I settled down to wait.

A couple of minutes later my mobile phone rang. Answering it, I heard nothing but heavy breathing. Deep, panting breaths. I was sitting there in the dark, alone in the car park, listening to a heavy breathing phone call from a pervert. Hastily, I locked the car doors.

Suddenly, to my immense relief, I heard a familiar voice at the other end of the phone.

"So sorry, Helen! I forgot about our early lesson and" (pause for more laboured breathing) "I went for my usual early morning run and..." (more panting) "I'm SO sorry – but I can't be there for seven-thirty - can I see you in about twenty minutes?"...

It has often been said (with good reason) that one should never assume anything. I was soon to learn the truth of this maxim.

All the French people I had met until now made a huge thing of their *Fête Nationale*. Every year on July 14th, they would celebrate

Bastille Day with great gusto and copious quantities of alcohol. Gloriously drunk, they would slap each other on the back with cries of *"vive la République!"* All jolly good fun – although it sometimes seemed to me a little bloodthirsty to be celebrating vast numbers of people (albeit the despised aristocracy) having their heads lopped off by the guillotine.

During the few days following the *Fête Nationale* all my students were normally eager to tell me what they had been up to on the public holiday. Parties, outings, family get-togethers – no matter how they had spent it, they would have been celebrating. And they were always keen to talk about it during their lesson.

Not so my delightful student. I was rather surprised. Surely he hadn't been so drunk that he had forgotten the celebrations already, I wondered, sitting opposite him a couple of days after the holiday. Puzzled, I prompted him.

"What did you do," I asked encouragingly, "to celebrate Bastille Day?"

There was a moment's hesitation, followed by a polite "er, nothing."

I should have left it there. I wish I had. Like an idiot, I ploughed on.

"Didn't you have a little family party or something? Just to mark the occasion?"

To his eternal credit, he answered me with the greatest courtesy and tact. The boyish grin this time was rather a rueful one.

"We don't actually celebrate July 14th in my family," he told me. "You see, my ancestors were members of the aristocracy."

Oops.

As mentioned before, I have occasionally taught groups of students, and my favourite of these by a mile was one of the DGA groups. The DGA is the French equivalent of our Ministry of Defence and security there is of course extremely tight. It was almost an hour's drive from my home, and I always had to allow additional time for my car to be searched (albeit politely and quickly) by the armed guards on duty, before I could be allowed onto the premises. I would then stop at the office to hand over my passport in exchange for a visitor's badge (this was, in fact, fairly common practice in many big organisations) and to collect the key to the classroom which was on the other side of the campus. Driving to the other block of buildings and finding the right room, I would unlock the door and at last begin preparations for the arrival of my lovely students.

The particular group I mentioned was made up of eight male students, ranging in age from thirty-something to fifty-something. All were helpful, funny, courteous and hard-working. All treated me with great kindness, consideration and good humour. Some of them really were very attractive. Others were, quite frankly, just simply drop-dead gorgeous.

During my first lesson with a new student or group of students, one of the things I ask them to do is to describe their company or organisation, telling me a bit about their role in it and the work they do. Realising that this would not be appropriate in this environment, I suggested to them as delicately as possible that, given the nature of their work, perhaps they could just give me a general outline of the sort of tasks they had to undertake. I realised, I added hastily, that it was all high security stuff and they couldn't tell me any details.

One of the group, without missing a beat, replied for them all.

"Well, we *could* tell you," he said, "but then we would have to kill you."

Their sense of humour was never far from the surface and I often wondered whether it was in fact the serious nature of their work that made them this way, as a kind of self preservation. One morning I was told by one of them that his colleague sent apologies for today's lesson because of an emergency situation at work. I knew from the morning's news that events in war-torn Syria had escalated overnight – France's involvement and the attendant logistics meant one of my students had more pressing priorities that day than his English lesson.

One of the exercises all my students seem to enjoy is the discussion of national stereotypes. Even the most reserved people enter into this with great enthusiasm as we laugh together about common misconceptions and generalisations.

The DGA students were no exception, each member of the group eager to contribute to the discussion, which was even more hilarious than usual. The British, I was told, were regarded by other nations as appalling cooks, as well as being by nature very cool and reserved. They didn't speak to each other on the train, but hid behind their newspapers wearing moustaches and bowler hats ("and that's just the women" one of them declared, to shouts of mirth from his colleagues).

When I finally managed to speak without laughing, I asked them how they thought the French people were perceived by other nations. They had no difficulty with this question and the national stereotypes were eagerly trotted out. Foreigners, I was told, thought that all French people went around on bicycles, wearing berets and strings of onions. We all laughed uproariously at this hilarious prospect.

"And," said one of them, warming to the topic, "they call us Froggies!"

Yes, yes, the others backed him up. *Froggies! It's terrible!*

"That's true, it's terrible" their spokesman confirmed – "but," he added, determined to clarify the situation, "they only call us Froggies because they are jealous – because they all know we are the best loverrrs!"

The journey to the DGA was a long one and the security hoops

I had to jump through in order to actually reach the classroom were, of necessity, strict and time consuming. However, the rewards were great and this group will always be remembered with great affection.

Each morning I would welcome the students one by one and, as they signed the attendance sheet, they would ask me considerately whether there was anything I needed. Could they get me a coffee from the machine? Did I want any photocopying done? Could they set up the projector, the screen, the loud speakers for the audio lessons? Nothing was too much trouble. Surrounded by these kind and delightful guys, with accents to die for, I would often reflect that there were probably worse ways of earning a living.

It's a tough job, but – as they say – somebody has to do it.

CHAPTER FIVE

SAY WHAT YOU MEAN

I have mentioned before that I frequently made mistakes when speaking French, to the huge delight of my new friends who seemed to find this both amusing and endearing. Equally entertaining were some of the interesting variations on the English language that my students would treat me to. On some occasions it was extremely hard to remain professional, as I felt the giggles rising at some particularly unfortunate gaffe.

Some of these were down to mis-pronunciation, while others could be attributed to what are known in French as the *faux amis,* or false friends. These are words or phrases which have a certain meaning in French, while the same word in English means something totally different (*le bordel* in chapter three being a perfect example). This of course applied equally in reverse, as I discovered when I tried to get to grips with the French language and encountered words which simply didn't mean what I felt they should.

I will never forget the very nice student who gave me the shock of my life during one of his lessons. We had been discussing the internet and how useful it could be, for work, for information, for other interests. Where would we be without it?

Always keen to encourage students to express their opinions in English and to develop a discussion, I asked him what sort of site he used most on the internet.

"Online bonking," he replied without hesitation.

Surely I had misheard him.

"Online – er...?" I quavered weakly.

"Bonking," he replied firmly.

Trying desperately to banish all thoughts of French porn websites from my mind, I wished heartily that I had never introduced this subject.

Seeing my confused expression, the student was beginning to explain. I wasn't at all sure this was a good idea.

"It's much easier than the normal sort of bonking," he began, to my dismay. "It saves you having to go into the town. In fact," he added helpfully, "you should try it yourself. You can transfer money and check your account online – you don't have to wait to get your bonk statement in the post!"

Ah. *That* sort of bonking. Phew...

One thing that all my students have found inordinately amusing is the number of words and phrases English speaking people have "borrowed" from the French language. In the interests of fairness, I would point out the equal number of our words that the French have "borrowed" and this would often lead to some good discussions.

Words like *le shopping* and *le weekend* are now part of everyday language in France. There are, of course, the purists who still insist on saying *fin de la semaine* (which in fact is what I was taught at school) and lecture anyone who will listen about the infiltration of these dreadful English words into their beautiful language. But language is a living thing, constantly evolving, and there was not much that could be done about it. A French politician started a campaign some years ago urging his compatriots to keep the French language "pure", but I believe this idea was greeted with typical Gallic shrugs and nobody really paid him much attention.

There were some words, I discovered, which had been "borrowed" from English and then changed slightly – or used to mean something not quite the same. This often led to confusion on the student's part because they were, after all, using an English word and could not understand why their English teacher didn't have the faintest idea what they were talking about.

One of my students told me about her son's birthday. He had received many nice presents, she told me, including a pair of baskets.

This puzzled me – I didn't imagine a teenage boy would be too interested in *le shopping* – so I asked her, curiously, what sort of baskets they were.

She looked surprised and told me they were the usual sort of baskets, the same as all the kids have these days.

Still none the wiser, I probed a little further. What will he put in these new baskets? I asked.

She looked at me as if I had gone mad.

"Well – his feet, of course!" she said, as if this was the most obvious thing in the world.

And, of course, it was. I discovered that *baskets* is the word used in French for sports shoes or trainers. Named after the game of basketball... We live and learn.

Conversely, I had never realised just how much of my own language was rooted in French until I worked as an English teacher. I remember one student telling me of an experience she had just had, which felt exactly the same as something that had happened before.

"In French," she told me, "we call this feeling *déjà vu*. What do you call it in English?"

Being philosophical about something, another student once told me "*c'est la vie* – well that's what we say in French..." etc.

Students would talk to me about leaving their children in a *crèche* when they came to work, and would ask for the English translation, looking disbelievingly at me when I explained that we used that word too.

I have made, on occasion – and no doubt still make – some mistakes in my attempts to speak French which are so hilarious, and are etched so clearly in my memory, that even now I blush with embarrassment at the mere recollection of them. Here are a few examples.

On arrival at my permanent home in Brittany, I started my new life with no furniture except for an ancient futon-style chair and a small coffee table. At least, I reasoned, I would have something to sit and sleep on and something to eat from – but clearly a few more bits and pieces would soon be needed.

I decided that buying a decent bed was a priority and went to a large furniture store, where I selected a double divan base which I was assured could be delivered to my home. The gentleman over there, I was told, could help me choose a suitable mattress.

What could possibly go wrong? Well, the answer to that question is that some French words sound (to me) so similar – especially as the last letter is invariably not pronounced – that I often find myself saying them incorrectly. The word for a mattress is, of course, *matelas*, while the word for a sailor is *matelot*.

To his credit, the young man in charge of mattresses was extremely polite and hid his surprise very well, but I'm sure he had fun telling the story to his colleagues after I had left. After all, it's not every day you get a strange English woman telling you she needs "a large sailor for her double bed"...

The plumber's wife was equally kind when my old central heating boiler *(chaudière)* broke down and I telephoned to explain to her that I had a "problem with my cauldron" *(chaudron)*.

Venturing into the fast diminishing number of shops where I had not yet embarrassed myself, I continued my quest for items for my new home, making heroic efforts to improve my pronunciation. So often, something as simple as distinguishing between a soft "g" and a hard "g" can make a huge difference in spoken French. On one notable occasion, I was seeking some ornamental candles (*bougies*, soft "g") to put in the lovely old sconces I had brought from England. The nice young man who served me must have been more than a little startled when I began describing the sort of "boogie" I would like him to show me, but dealt with the situation with commendable tact and courtesy. As I left, clutching a box of candles and the remaining shreds of my dignity, I mentally added yet another shop to my list of those to avoid in future.

The French language can indeed be a minefield and I still occasionally become confused by its own *faux amis* – the words that you feel really should mean something quite different. The innocent sounding *préservatif*, for example, turned out to be a condom. A *commode* was a chest of drawers. However, once I had grasped these basic facts, my jam-making efforts and furniture buying expeditions did become a little less stressful.

No doubt I have given a few people a few laughs along the way with my gaffes. Well, OK, perhaps quite a lot of laughs. We live and learn – and I, obviously, am still learning. Well, *c'est la vie* and we all make the occasional *faux pas*. Wonder how they say that in French?...

CHAPTER SIX

WITH A LITTLE HELP FROM MY FRIENDS

The importance of having good friends should never be underestimated and in this respect I have been exceptionally lucky. If my friends in England had any doubts about my sanity when I set off on this adventure, they kept them well hidden, giving me nothing but encouragement and support every step of the way. Old friends, colleagues, ex neighbours – all have stayed in touch, visited me and welcomed me warmly into their homes on my twice-yearly visits to the UK. My friends have shown me more love and loyalty than I could ever possibly deserve; they are, quite simply, the best.

In France, too, I have made friends, and have spent some wonderful times with them, but it is not quite the same. My French has improved, becoming faster and more colloquial, but it is still never easy to pour your heart out in a language other than your native tongue, or to follow the really rapid gabbling of some French conversations. That said, the friends I have made have been incredibly kind and welcoming to me, gently teasing me about my accent – "ha ha, you sound like Jane Birkin!" – and correcting my mistakes, helpfully teaching me the *gros mots* (rude words) "just in case I should ever use one unintentionally".

I met some lovely and interesting people through an organisation whose members arranged group events and get-togethers. There were theatre and cinema trips, walks and picnics, parties, visits to beautiful *châteaux* – and one unforgettable New Year's Eve spent in a yurt village near Saint-Malo. All were happy and enjoyable social events.

During this time, I went with groups on several occasions to visit the Mont St-Michel. It was a novelty to be there as a tourist, enjoying the chance to explore this special and breathtaking place at leisure, while the stuffing of baguettes was left to others...

The friends I made through these groups would also let me know if they heard of any events which might be of interest to me – in particular anything English-related.

On one occasion I was invited by some of these friends to a concert at their local church. This, they told me, was being put on by the local twinning association, of which they were members, together with the visiting choir from its twin town in Yorkshire. It was all free, would I like to come?

Not really expecting much, I turned up on the day and settled down on a hard wooden pew waiting for the concert to begin. To my surprise, I found the quality of the singing superb: French voices performing English songs, the English choir singing the French songs they had learnt... and then the two choirs together, their voices blending in a harmony so sweet that it brought tears to my eyes.

Afterwards, outside the church, my friends were eager to know my opinion. Had I enjoyed it? Yes, I told them emphatically, it was wonderful! Such excellent entertainment – and all free! In fact I would have been happy to pay for a ticket...

"You should have been here last time," they were saying, "when our choir sang the Yorkshire song!"

"Yorkshire song?" I asked, "which one?"

Well, they said, it was a very well known one – the visitors from Yorkshire had taught it to the French choir... and then the French choir performed it. You *must* know it, they said – it was something about being on the moor *sans chapeau*...

My mind, I have to say, boggled. French people, singing "On Ilkley Moor Baht 'At". With French accents.

Now *that*, believe me, is something I really would pay good money to hear.

For my teaching work and many other things, including the all-important e-mails, my computer was absolutely essential. That being so, I don't know what I would have done without my friend Computer Cathy.

Cathy, a cheerful divorcee with a heart of gold and an alarming number of grandchildren, ran her own IT troubleshooting service when I first met her socially. After closing down her business and going back on the "nine to five", she would still come to my house to look after my PC. Time and again, she nursed my elderly computer back to health – between fag breaks on the balcony – in return for nothing more than mates' rates and a pot of strong coffee. We also took the opportunity on these visits to *refaire le monde*, as she called it, or to put the world to rights.

One such occasion was June 24th 2016. Still reeling somewhat from the unexpected (to me) result of the EU Referendum which had just been announced, I opened the door to find Cathy with a stricken expression on her face. Hugging me to within an inch of my life, she began, *"Oh Hélène!"* and then launched into a tirade of French so rapid that all I could make out was the odd expletive and the words *Le Brexit*.

"Come in, Cathy," I said gently when she paused for breath, *"un petit café?"* Clearly coffee was called for immediately, the stronger the better.

"But what will you *do*?" she asked anxiously, recovering slightly and adding an extra lump of sugar to her cup. "What will happen to you and all the British people here? What will *become* of you?" And off she went again... Clearly *Le Brexit* was not flavour of the month.

"Don't worry," I told her, sounding more confident than I felt. "It will all be OK, I'm sure. *Ca ira.* Everything will be all right."

Cathy drained and refilled her coffee cup. She was calmer now, but still determined to have the last word on the subject. *"Les Anglais!"* she muttered darkly, with one of those Gallic shrugs I have come to know and love. *"Pffftt!!* ... Have they all gone raving mad over there?"

CHAPTER SEVEN

NEW BEGINNINGS AGAIN

Raving mad or not, I will always be British and, wherever I may travel, England – the country of my birth – will always be very special to me. It saddened me on my arrival in France to hear so many British ex-pats comparing the UK unfavourably with France. Everything in France, if you believed them, was wonderful – better, cheaper, more enjoyable. By contrast, everything in the UK was rubbish. The idea that you could appreciate two different countries and cultures simply hadn't occurred to them – loving France and loving the UK was, to their mind, impossible. The two things were mutually exclusive.

To my mind, this was never the case. There were things I loved doing in the UK that I missed when I came to live in France. Likewise, on my return - which I am now planning - there will be things about France that I will miss very much too. However, short of winning the Lottery (and it might help if I bought a ticket) having a home in both countries will never be an option for me. With retirement approaching, some serious thinking was needed about where I would be able to enjoy my new-found freedom to the full. I dearly love rural Brittany and the peace and solitude it offers – as a place to come home to after a day working in Rennes, for example, it is a haven of tranquility. Now, though, I am ready to give up work and, as my thoughts turn to having fun and a more fulfilling social life, it is the UK that ticks all the boxes for me. Best of all, I can spend my retirement closer to my family and friends. I have known in my heart for some time that this would ultimately be my choice – and now I believe the right time has come to start that new adventure.

Of one thing I am sure – coming to live in France is something I will always be so glad I did. My experiences here have been many and varied – good, bad and sometimes unbelievable (the attitude to vegetarians and the casual sexism falling into the latter category!) There have been huge challenges at times and I have learnt a lot – about France, about the French people, about the kindness of strangers... and about myself. I have learnt about my own strengths and weaknesses and have occasionally surprised myself with my own resilience. It has been a fascinating, positive and often humbling experience.

There are so many things about France that I will miss when I go back – and others that I will not miss, just as the same could be said about the UK when I left there thirteen years ago.

Living in the countryside, I have become so much more aware of the changing of the seasons, even the phases of the moon, which often passed unnoticed before. With no light pollution in this lovely rural area, the sight of the moon and stars etched brightly in a black velvet sky is one that still takes my breath away and is something I will never forget. Equally breathtaking are the spectacular electric storms that split the night sky with their jagged forked lightning and rattle my windows with deafening cracks of thunder.

The gentler sounds of the countryside here have always enchanted me. Falling asleep to the sound of owls calling softly and the distant barking of a vixen protecting her cubs is, quite simply, magical. All these things are the normal background sounds to life here and I have probably come to take them for granted – but I know that I will miss them when they are no longer there.

I will always remember Brittany for its wonderful *crêperies*, where even a vegetarian can get the most delicious food and eat very cheaply. The large *galettes*, pancakes made with the local *blé noir* (buckwheat flour), are served with a huge choice of fillings and, accompanied by a carafe of scrumptious Breton cider or good red wine, make one of my favourite meals. Followed - if you have room - by one of the more delicate *crêpes* served for dessert, with cream and fruit or caramel ice-cream with toffee sauce, the experience is a gastronomic delight. When I first discovered *crêperies* I thought I had gone to heaven.

I will always remember celebrating Midnight Mass with French friends one Christmas Eve in the majestic mediaeval Abbey perched on top of the mystical Mont St-Michel. A French person once told me "this is a place with its own soul" and I know exactly what she meant.

I will remember the exciting (and very choppy!) boat trip from Granville to the Isles de Chausey, off the coast of Normandy, to celebrate my sixtieth birthday with friends, French and English. We spent the day on the *Grande Isle*, the largest island but still tiny, a beautiful spot with its fortress, chapel, small hotel, sandy beaches and flock of black sheep. My friends brought champagne and we drank it from paper cups with our picnic lunch.

I will miss the beautiful surroundings in my hamlet and waking to silence except for the sound of birdsong. I will miss the creamy walnuts from my garden and the sweet yellow plums that grow faster than I can pick them. I will miss the space and the tranquillity.

In spite of all the things I will miss, it will be wonderful to have public transport again (noticeable here by its complete absence), to be able to visit more frequently the people I love most, to walk to the shops and to have a choice of entertainment – to join the "mainstream" of life again, in a world which is familiar but also in some ways strange to me now. The new life that awaits me will have its own joys and, no doubt, its own challenges.

Among the things I will not miss (and neither will my cats) is *la Chasse*, the weekly hunt that takes place during autumn and winter in the neighbouring countryside. I am aware of the damage foxes can cause to poultry and other livestock and I do appreciate the need to cull the fox population. However, the *chasseurs'* habit of taking pot shots at anything that moves, including domestic animals (and according to my neighbours, boasting and laughing about it afterwards) means that all pets must be confined to barracks every Sunday, for several months each year. I have heard so many sad stories of animals which have come to grief through not being kept safe indoors that I now insist on the cat-flap remaining firmly locked on hunting days, despite loud protests and mutinous looks from my four-legged friends.

Ironically, I will never know whether it was a fox or the hunters themselves who took my little black and white cat, Merlin, some years ago – or whether some other fate befell him. This was a cat whose brazenness knew no bounds (to my acute embarrassment he would turn up uninvited at the neighbours' barbecues, waiting politely to be served along with the other guests). He was gifted with an ability to charm the birds from the trees – and the bats, and... well, you get the picture. His thirst for adventure was unquenchable. So although he may have met with a sad end, he may equally have simply stowed away in the back of someone's car or van – another favourite trick of his – and taken up residence with a new family. If so, I'm sure they have enjoyed his company as much as I did – and they will doubtless have been grateful for his prowess as a prolific mouser.

Old friends Pip and Lucy are now laid to rest, beneath the willow tree on my sunny terrace. With them is Daisy, my pretty little French cat, who was hit by a car, down by the granite quarry, at just two years old. Sweet dreams, my beautiful girls. Wherever I may be, a part of me will always stay here with you.

The present incumbents, Misty and Mégane, are known to friends as "the hooligan twins" and make every effort to live up to their name. As I write, they are jumping in and out of a large cardboard box which I had intended to fill with books. I remember when they were tiny kittens, how their favourite game was to hide and jump out at each other, purring with excitement.

Misty and Mégane, along with three other siblings, were found by an English lady and her dog. They had been placed in a bag and left in a ditch at the age of around four weeks old. Miraculously rescued and lovingly nurtured, all five survived and homes were found for them all.

Following an initial "Mexican stand-off" (with old Pip making it clear she would really prefer her house not to be invaded by two young upstarts) peace finally reigned. My lovely old cat carried out her role as adoptive mum with great tenderness (and the occasional clip round the ear when she deemed it necessary). By contrast to their appalling start in life, Misty and Mégane have lived the lives of minor royalty since the day I brought them home. They seem to regard this as nothing more than their due – and to be honest, all in all, I am inclined to agree with them.

What will they make of this new adventure? A new country, a new home... Knowing them, I think the hooligan twins will throw themselves into it all with the same enthusiasm they have for everything. As long as they have a garden to play in and a lap to snuggle up on, they will be happy. They are contented souls and they, like me, get great enjoyment from the simple pleasures in life.

So many memories, so many emotions. It is the end of an era, yes – but also the beginning of an exciting new one. My friends here – French, English, Dutch – will, I am sure, stay in touch and I hope they will visit me when they can. I will come back to Brittany and see them whenever possible. As Patrick once said, this is not *"adieu"*, only *"au revoir"*.

No more daydreaming! – it's time to turf the cats out of that box, fill it with books and prepare to get the show on the road...

Now where did I put that spotted handkerchief?

Printed in Great Britain
by Amazon

30842719R00030